TERRELL WINTON

The Way of Wisdom: 31 Days Through The Book of Proverbs

Copyright © 2025 by Terrell Winton

All rights reserved. No part of this publication may be reproduced, stored or transmitted in any form or by any means, electronic, mechanical, photocopying, recording, scanning, or otherwise without written permission from the publisher. It is illegal to copy this book, post it to a website, or distribute it by any other means without permission.

First edition

This book was professionally typeset on Reedsy.
Find out more at reedsy.com

Contents

Acknowledgments		v
Introduction		1
1	Day 1 – The Beginning of Wisdom	2
2	Day 2 – Trust in the Lord	5
3	Day 3 – Trust In The Lord	8
4	Day 4 – The Power of Words	11
5	Day 5 – Walking With the Wise	14
6	Day 6 – The Reward of Diligence	17
7	Day 7 – The Blessing of Generosity	20
8	Day 8 – Humility Before Honor	23
9	Day 9 – The Name of the Lord	26
10	Day 10 – Discipline as Love	29
11	Day 11 – The Plans of the Heart	32
12	Day 12 – Wise Counsel	34
13	Day 13 – A Cheerful Heart	37
14	Day 14 – Wisdom and Wealth	40
15	Day 15 – A Soft Answer	43
16	Day 16 – Commit Your Works	46
17	Day 17 – Guard your Tongue	49
18	Day 18 – Humility Over Pride	52
19	Day 19 – The Power of Generational Legacy	55
20	Day 20 – The Blessing of Righteousness	58
21	Day 21 – The Power Of Self Control	61
22	Day 22 – The Wisdom of Patience	64
23	Day 23 – Guarding Against Envy	66
24	Day 24 – Honoring Generational Wisdom	68

25	Day 25 – Speaking Truth in Love	71
26	Day 26 – The Power of Planning	74
27	Day 27 – Friendships & Iron Sharpens Iron	77
28	Day 28 – God Directs the Steps	79
29	Day 29 – A Good Name	82
30	Day 30 – The Boldness of the Righteous	84
31	Day 31 – Wisdom Crowned	86
32	Closing Words	88
33	Reader's Blessing – A Prayer of Wisdom	90
	About the Author	92

Acknowledgments

First, to the Spirit of Wisdom Himself — thank you for speaking, teaching, and stretching me until these words came alive.

To my wife, Kristyn — thank you for praying, warring, laughing, and laboring with me in every season. Together we are building a legacy that will outlive us.

To my children — you are arrows in the hand of a warrior. May this book water seeds of destiny in you.

To my mentors and apostolic covering — thank you for teaching me that wisdom is imparted, not just taught.

And to every reader — you are not holding a book, you are holding strategy for your future. May these words ignite your path.

Introduction

Welcome to The Way of Wisdom. This is not just a devotional — it's a divine summons. Proverbs is not casual reading; it is kingdom instruction. Every line carries strategy for life, warfare against foolishness, and the keys to longevity, favor, and victory.

Wisdom is not optional for the believer. It is the Spirit's advantage system — the edge God gives you to live above the structures of this world. Flesh will always try to convince you that your way is better, that shortcuts will prosper, and that comfort is safer. But wisdom calls you higher.

Over these next 31 days, you will not just read words; you will encounter the Spirit of Wisdom. You will be stretched, corrected, strengthened, and equipped to walk with God in a way that secures your future and reshapes your legacy.

This is a prophetic journey. Some days will confront you. Others will heal you. All of them will move you forward.

Your brightest days are not behind you — they are ahead. In the name of Jesus, I declare that as you read, wisdom will crown your head, guard your path, and establish your destiny.

— Terrell Winton

1

Day 1 – The Beginning of Wisdom

Scripture:
"The reverent and worshipful fear of the Lord is the beginning and the principal and choice part of knowledge, but fools despise skillful and godly Wisdom, instruction, and discipline." (Proverbs 1:7, AMPC)

Teaching

Every structure needs a foundation, and Proverbs makes it clear: the foundation of wisdom is the **fear of the Lord.** Not terror, but reverence. Awe. A holy recognition that God is God, and we are not.

This is more than intellectual agreement — it is posture. To fear the Lord is to center Him in every decision, to acknowledge His ways above our ways, and to recognize that apart from Him, all "wisdom" is folly.

Flesh will always resist this. Flesh says: *"I can figure it out. I don't need counsel. My way is better."* But Scripture calls that foolishness. To despise instruction is to despise safety. To resist wisdom is to reject protection.

Here's the wisdom principle: **the fear of the Lord is not the end of wisdom; it is the entry point.**

Counseling Insight

In counseling, I often find people trying to build their lives without foundation. They gather knowledge — podcasts, books, advice from friends — but knowledge without the fear of the Lord produces instability. It's like decorating the walls of a house with no concrete slab beneath it. Eventually, the cracks show.

When you reframe life decisions through reverence — "What does God say about this? How can I honor Him here?" — wisdom begins to flow, and what was shaky becomes secure.

Story

I remember in my own life facing a season where I thought I had it figured out. I was chasing opportunities and leaning hard on my own strategy. Outwardly, it looked good. Inwardly, I was exhausted. It wasn't until I stopped and admitted, *"Lord, I've been trying to build without You,"* that things shifted. When I humbled myself, wisdom showed up like a flood. What felt confusing became clear.

Application

- Begin every day with reverence: "God, You are God, and I am not."
- Before making decisions, pause to ask: "What honors God here?"
- Treat correction not as rejection but as protection.

Reflection Prompts

1. Where have I tried to build without a foundation of reverence?
2. How do I usually respond to correction — with humility or resistance?
3. What would shift if I truly made God the beginning of every decision?

Prayer

Lord, I humble myself before You today. Teach me the fear of the Lord. Help me to walk in awe, reverence, and surrender. Guard me from foolishness, and let wisdom be my foundation. Amen.

Prophetic Decree

In the name of Jesus, I decree that the fear of the Lord will be established in you as a foundation that cannot be shaken. You will not build on sand, but on the Rock. Wisdom will meet you at the entryway of reverence, and your life will stand secure.

2

Day 2 - Trust in the Lord

Scripture:
"Keep and guard your heart with all vigilance and above all that you guard, for out of it flow the springs of life." (Proverbs 4:23, AMPC)

Teaching

If Day 1 taught us that wisdom begins with reverence for the Lord, Day 2 shows us where that wisdom must dwell: the heart. Solomon, writing to his son, doesn't say *guard your money, your reputation, or your possessions.* He says guard your **heart** — because everything else flows from there.

The Hebrew word for heart here is **"lev"** (לֵב), which doesn't just mean emotions. It represents the inner man — the seat of thought, will, emotions, and spirit. In other words, your heart is the control center of your life.

Why guard it? Because your heart is both a gateway and a reservoir. Whatever enters your heart has the power to shape your actions, attitudes, and destiny. If bitterness, fear, and pride are allowed in, they become the waters you drink from daily. But if love, faith, and the Word of God fill it, then what flows out will be life-giving.

Jesus echoed this in **Luke 6:45**: *"The good man out of the good treasure of his heart brings forth what is good... for his mouth speaks from the overflow of his heart."* Your words, your decisions, even your relationships — they are all downstream from the condition of your heart.

But here's where wisdom as a **heavenly advantage** comes in: you are not left to guard your heart in your own strength. The Holy Spirit gives discernment — that *inner check* when something is not healthy for your spirit. Paul calls it the *peace of Christ* that acts as a "umpire" in our hearts (**Colossians 3:15**). This means wisdom is not only knowledge but protection — a Spirit-empowered alarm system for your inner life.

When you yield to the Spirit, wisdom alerts you: *"Don't let that conversation in." "Don't let that fear linger." "Don't let that toxic relationship settle in your soul."* This is the **heavenly advantage** at work. While the world tries to cope with stress, trauma, and toxic environments, the Spirit empowers you to guard your heart so that what flows from it remains life.

Application

Guarding your heart requires vigilance. You cannot be passive. Just as a security guard is positioned at a door to determine who comes in, you must actively discern what you allow into your mind and spirit.

Some practical ways this plays out:

- **Guard your inputs.** What are you reading, watching, or listening to? Everything you consume either deposits life or drains it.
- **Guard your relationships.** Who has access to your inner circle? Proverbs 13:20 warns that the companion of fools suffers harm. Wisdom means setting boundaries without guilt.
- **Guard your identity.** Don't let lies from the enemy take root. Replace them with God's truth.

The Spirit's role is essential here. Without Him, guarding your heart feels like striving or self-policing. With Him, you walk in discernment, and wisdom becomes the filter that allows life to flow freely.

Reflection Prompts

1. What patterns, habits, or relationships have I allowed to shape my heart that I need to release?
2. Where do I sense the Spirit urging me to set stronger boundaries?
3. How can I create more space in my heart for God's Word to dwell richly?

Prayer/Declaration

Father, I thank You for the gift of wisdom and the power of Your Spirit that enables me to guard my heart. Teach me to discern what belongs and what does not. I declare that my heart is a wellspring of life, not of bitterness or fear. I choose to let Your Word and Your Spirit guard the gates of my inner life, so that everything that flows out of me brings life to others. Amen.

3

Day 3 – Trust In The Lord

Scripture: *"Lean on, trust in, and be confident in the Lord with all your heart and mind and do not rely on your own insight or understanding. In all your ways know, recognize, and acknowledge Him, and He will direct and make straight and plain your paths."* (Proverbs 3:5–6, AMPC)

Teaching

Few verses in Proverbs are as quoted as this one, yet few are as deeply wrestled with. We love the promise — God directing our paths — but often resist the condition: surrendering our trust.

The Hebrew word for "trust" here is **"batach" (חָטַב)**, which carries the sense of throwing yourself down upon, lying helpless, or putting full weight on something. It's not partial confidence; it's full reliance. Solomon doesn't say, "Trust God with most of your heart." He says, "with *all* your heart and mind."

That means no backup plans, no half measures, no silent "just in case" safety nets. True wisdom recognizes that our understanding, no matter how sharp, is finite. The Hebrew word for "understanding" is **"binah" (הָנִיב)**, meaning discernment, perception, or insight. Our binah is limited. God's wisdom is infinite.

Here's where the revelation deepens: **flesh isn't skin and bones. Flesh is sense and reason without the influence of the Holy Spirit.** This is why Solomon warns us, *"do not rely on your own understanding."* Your flesh will always try to convince you that your way is better, that comfort and convenience will bring greater returns. But that's a lie. Flesh seeks shortcuts. Flesh values ease over obedience. Flesh promises results without cost. But wisdom says: God's way is higher, even if it looks harder at first.

Paul described this tension in **Romans 8:6**: *"For the mind of the flesh is death, but the mind of the [Holy] Spirit is life and peace."* When you lean on your own reasoning apart from the Spirit, it may feel logical, but it leads to frustration, disappointment, or even destruction. When you lean into the Spirit, you tap into life, peace, and divine direction.

Trust, then, is not abandoning reason — it's refusing to let reason rule apart from the Spirit. Trust is choosing the **heavenly advantage system** over the flesh's limited and deceptive reasoning.

Application

Trusting God is not passive. It requires action — the daily choice to silence the voice of flesh and amplify the voice of the Spirit. Flesh will always say, *"Do what feels safe. Choose what looks easy. Pick what's comfortable."* But wisdom knows that the Spirit often leads us into the unfamiliar, the inconvenient, and the stretching — because that's where God's greater purpose is revealed.

Every time you choose trust over flesh, you are declaring: *"I will not be ruled by my limited understanding; I will be led by the Spirit of God."* That is where wisdom flourishes.

1. **Lean not on your own understanding.** Ask yourself: am I relying more on my calculations than on God's leading? Wisdom says: yield.
2. **In all your ways acknowledge Him.** Acknowledge means to "know intimately" (Hebrew: **yada**). Trust isn't just saying "God, bless my plans." It's submitting every decision — big and small — to His lordship.
3. **He will direct your paths.** The result of trust is direction. The word

"direct" here means to make straight, to clear obstacles, to prepare the road. Trust doesn't mean life will be easy, but it means your steps will be ordered.

Trusting God may feel risky, but the real risk is living without His direction.

Reflection Prompts

1. Where in my life am I leaning more on my own understanding than on God's wisdom?
2. What step of trust is the Spirit inviting me to take right now?
3. How would my decisions change if I treated the Spirit's guidance as my greatest advantage?

Prayer/Declaration

Father, I release the need to control and the fear of the unknown. I lean wholly on You, knowing that Your Spirit sees what I cannot. Today I choose to acknowledge You in every decision. I declare that my steps are ordered, my paths are straightened, and my future is aligned with Your perfect will. Amen.

.

4

Day 4 – The Power of Words

Scripture: *"Death and life are in the power of the tongue, and they who indulge in it shall eat the fruit of it [for death or life]."*(Proverbs 18:21, AMPC)

Teaching

Words are not neutral. Every word carries weight — either releasing life or ushering in death. Solomon reminds us here that our tongue is not just for communication; it is a creative force.

The Hebrew word for "power" here is **"yad" (יָד)**, meaning *hand, strength, or authority.* In other words, your tongue holds authority — it is the *hand of your spirit.* What you release with your mouth has the ability to shape reality, to frame atmospheres, and to influence destinies.

James builds on this truth in **James 3:5–6**, where he compares the tongue to a small spark that can set an entire forest ablaze. A few words can destroy a relationship, crush a dream, or ignite division. But in the same way, a few words can heal, inspire, and restore.

Here's the key: the tongue will always echo whichever realm you're yielded to — flesh or Spirit. **Flesh is sense and reason without the influence of the Spirit.** And flesh loves to talk. It will justify anger, magnify fear, and spread doubt. Flesh convinces you that venting, gossiping, or complaining are harmless — but in reality, those words carry the fragrance of death.

But when the Spirit governs your tongue, your words become carriers of heaven. Jesus said in **John 6:63**, *"The words I speak to you are spirit and they are life."* Spirit-filled words do more than encourage — they release divine power into situations. When you declare God's Word over your life, your family, or your community, you are not speaking empty phrases — you are partnering with heaven to shift realities on earth.

This is why wisdom teaches us to guard our speech. Words spoken in the flesh trap us in cycles of frustration. Words released by the Spirit align us with kingdom breakthrough. Wisdom is knowing the difference.

Application

Every believer must choose daily: will my tongue echo the reasoning of flesh or the revelation of the Spirit?

- **In conflict,** flesh wants to retaliate. Spirit empowers you to speak peace.
- **In discouragement,** flesh speaks doubt. Spirit empowers you to declare hope.
- **In uncertainty,** flesh speaks fear. Spirit empowers you to declare faith.

This is not about pretending everything is fine — it's about choosing to align your speech with truth greater than what you see. When you consistently speak Spirit-led words, you're not only protecting your own atmosphere — you're shaping the environment of everyone around you.

Words are seeds. What you speak today is what you will eat tomorrow. That's why Solomon says we "eat the fruit" of our words. If you don't like the harvest you're experiencing, change the seed you're planting.

Reflection Prompts

1. Where in my life do I notice my tongue echoing the reasoning of flesh rather than the revelation of the Spirit?
2. What negative or careless words have I been planting, and what life-

giving words can I sow instead?
3. How can I be more intentional about speaking God's promises over my life, family, and purpose?

Prayer/Declaration

Holy Spirit, take control of my tongue. I repent for words spoken in the flesh — words of doubt, fear, or destruction. Today, I choose to align my speech with Your truth. I declare that my words carry life, my declarations shift atmospheres, and my tongue is an instrument of wisdom and breakthrough. In Jesus' name, Amen.

5

Day 5 – Walking With the Wise

Scripture: *"He who walks with wise men will be wise, but the companion of fools will smart for it."* (Proverbs 13:20, AMPC)

Teaching

Wisdom is not only received by revelation — it is caught by association. Solomon reminds us here that who you walk with determines what you become.

The Hebrew word for "walks" is **"halak"** (הָלַךְ), meaning to journey, to live out, or to follow a path together. This isn't about casual acquaintances — it's about those you share life with, those who shape your thinking, those whose voices you allow closest to your heart.

In ancient Jewish culture, this truth was lived out in the way disciples followed their rabbis. A rabbi didn't just teach in a classroom — he lived with his students, and they followed him everywhere. The Mishnah uses the phrase: *"Cover yourself in the dust of their feet."* This meant that a disciple should walk so closely behind his rabbi that the dust from his sandals would settle on him.

To walk with a rabbi wasn't only to learn his words — it was to absorb his life. His wisdom became your wisdom. His way became your way. This is the image Proverbs paints: to walk with the wise is to be covered in their dust, shaped by their example until wisdom seeps into you.

This is why Jesus called His disciples not only to listen but to follow Him. And even more — He gave them His Spirit, so that His wisdom could dwell inside of them. When we walk with the Spirit, we aren't just following behind a rabbi; we are indwelt by the Rabbi Himself, Christ our wisdom (1 Cor. 1:30).

The flip side is equally true. To walk with fools is to inherit their dust — their habits, their dysfunction, their rebellion. Their dust settles on you, and soon, you're walking in patterns that aren't your own.

Wisdom, then, is choosing whose dust you're willing to wear.

Application

Walking with the wise requires intentionality. You cannot choose your family, but you can choose your mentors, your friends, and your inner circle.

Ask yourself:

- **Who are the voices I've given authority in my life?** Do they align with the Spirit's wisdom or with fleshly reasoning?
- **Am I walking with those who challenge me to grow, or those who keep me comfortable in mediocrity?**
- **Do I surround myself with people who fear the Lord, or those who despise instruction?**

The Spirit will sometimes nudge you to create distance from certain relationships — not out of arrogance, but out of protection. This is wisdom guarding your destiny. And at the same time, the Spirit will highlight those you should draw near to — spiritual mentors, kingdom-minded peers, or even those you are called to disciple.

Wisdom knows that association is impartation.

Reflection Prompts

1. Who are the three voices that influence me most right now — and are they wise or foolish?
2. How has my environment shaped my decision-making, for better or worse?
3. Who do I need to intentionally walk with in this season to grow in Spirit-led wisdom?

Prayer/Declaration

Lord, open my eyes to see the relationships that sharpen me and the ones that dull me. Give me courage to walk with the wise and discernment to distance myself from foolishness. Surround me with Spirit-filled voices that align with Your kingdom, and make me one who carries wisdom for others. Amen.

6

Day 6 – The Reward of Diligence

Scripture: *"He becomes poor who works with a slack and idle hand, but the hand of the diligent makes rich."* (Proverbs 10:4, AMPC)

Teaching

Solomon reminds us that wisdom is not just about what we *know* but about what we *do*. Here, diligence is contrasted with laziness, showing us that the fruit of our lives often reflects the posture of our hands.

The Hebrew word for "slack" is **"remiyyah"** (הָרְמִיָּה), which means deceitful, negligent, or idle. It paints the picture of a hand that doesn't follow through, a worker who starts but doesn't finish, or someone who avoids effort altogether. In contrast, "diligent" is **"charuts"** (חָרוּץ), which means sharp, decisive, determined. It's not just busyness; it's focused, consistent effort with purpose.

In the ancient world, particularly in agricultural societies like Israel, laziness was not just a personal flaw — it was dangerous. ...

But here's the deeper truth: sometimes what looks like laziness is actually **procrastination — and procrastination is a spirit.** It disguises itself as delay, distraction, or indecision, but its root is fear. Fear of failure. Fear of success. Fear of responsibility. Fear that you're not enough, or fear of what will happen if you actually are enough.

Procrastination is subtle because it feels safer to "wait until later" than to risk obedience today. But what it really does is choke out diligence and abort harvests. Proverbs warns us that "hope deferred makes the heart sick" (Prov. 13:12), and procrastination is one of the enemy's most effective tools for endless deferral.

This is why diligence requires the Spirit. Flesh gives in to fear; the Spirit gives power, love, and a sound mind (2 Tim. 1:7). The Spirit exposes the root cause of procrastination, heals the fear behind it, and empowers you to cultivate consistency, focus, and endurance.

Application

Diligence is not about gritting your teeth harder — it's about confronting what holds you back.

- **Identify the root.** Ask: *Why do I struggle with follow-through here?* Is it fear of failure? Fear of people's opinions? Fear of responsibility?
- **Bring it to God.** Fear loses power when it's named and surrendered. Ask the Spirit to replace fear with boldness.
- **Practice small consistencies.** Start with one small area and be faithful in it. Faithfulness in little builds capacity for much.

When procrastination is broken, diligence can flourish. And when diligence flourishes, wisdom leads you into harvest.

Practical examples:

- In your **calling,** diligence is stewarding your gifts and preparing even when doors haven't opened yet.
- In your **finances,** diligence is budgeting, saving, and giving faithfully, not waiting for "one big break."
- In your **spiritual life,** diligence is prayer, study, and worship, even when you don't feel like it.

DAY 6 – THE REWARD OF DILIGENCE

The reward of diligence is not just financial prosperity — though Proverbs acknowledges that it often brings increase. The deeper reward is spiritual growth, credibility, and capacity. Diligence enlarges you to handle more, while laziness shrinks your influence.

Reflection Prompts

1. Where have I allowed fleshly comfort or convenience to make me slack with what God has placed in my hands?
2. What assignment or discipline is the Spirit calling me to re-engage with diligence?
3. How can I cultivate consistency, focus, and endurance in this season?

Prayer/Declaration

Father, I thank You that You have entrusted me with gifts, assignments, and opportunities. Forgive me for the times I've allowed laziness or distraction to rob me of harvest. Today, I receive the Spirit's power to walk in diligence. I declare that my hands are strong, my focus is sharp, and my consistency produces fruit that honors You. Amen.

7

Day 7 – The Blessing of Generosity

Scripture: *"The liberal person shall be enriched, and he who waters shall himself be watered."* (Proverbs 11:25, AMPC)

Teaching

The wisdom of Proverbs often confronts the wisdom of the world. The world says: *"Hold tightly to what you have, protect your own, save for yourself."* But Proverbs reveals a kingdom paradox: the one who gives freely is the one who receives abundantly.

The Hebrew word for "liberal" here is **"berakah"** (הְכָרְב), meaning *blessing, prosperity, generous.* It describes not just someone who gives occasionally, but a person whose lifestyle is generosity. The image is of an open hand rather than a closed fist.

The second half of the verse is agricultural imagery: *"he who waters shall himself be watered."* In ancient Israel, where water was precious and life-sustaining, irrigation was both costly and essential. To water someone else's field meant sacrificing your own resources. But Solomon promises that when you refresh others, God Himself ensures that refreshment comes back to you.

Here's the deeper truth: generosity is not a transaction — it is a spiritual principle. Paul echoes this in **2 Corinthians 9:6**: *"Whoever sows sparingly will also reap sparingly, and whoever sows generously will also reap generously."* Generosity aligns you with the flow of heaven. God is a giver by nature, and when you give, you step into His rhythm.

And generosity is not just about money. It's about all the resources God has entrusted to you — your time, your energy, your wisdom, your relationships, your compassion. All of it comes from Him. When you withhold it, when you hoard what was meant to flow through you, you silently agree with the world's broken system of scarcity.

This broken system is what Jesus confronted in **Matthew 16:25**: *"For whoever desires to save his life will lose it, but whoever loses his life for My sake will find it."* The world says: *"Keep, save, protect, hoard."* But the kingdom says: *"Release, sow, pour out — and in losing, you find true life."*

Generosity, then, is not loss — it is alignment with God's system of abundance. Every time you give, you declare: *"I will not agree with scarcity; I will agree with heaven's overflow."*

Application

Generosity is not about how much you have; it's about how much you're willing to release. Wisdom doesn't measure generosity by the size of the gift but by the posture of the heart.

Practical steps of Spirit-led generosity:

- **Be open-handed with people.** Encourage, mentor, pray for, and invest in others. Your time is often more valuable than your money.
- **Give beyond comfort.** If generosity never stretches you, it's not costing you anything. Sacrificial giving invites supernatural return.
- **Refresh intentionally.** Look for ways to water others — speak life, give resources, meet needs — and trust that God will water you in return.

Generosity breaks the spirit of poverty and fear because it declares: *"My source is not what's in my hand, but who's in my life."*

Reflection Prompts

1. Do I approach generosity from a place of fear (flesh) or trust (Spirit)?
2. Who in my life can I intentionally "water" this week?
3. How have I seen God refresh me when I've chosen to refresh others?

Prayer/Declaration

Father, thank You for being my source and supply. I repent for the times I have withheld out of fear or selfishness. Today I choose to walk in Spirit-led generosity. I declare that as I water others, I will be watered. As I release what You've entrusted to me, I step into the flow of Your blessing. My hands are open, and my life overflows with generosity. Amen.

8

Day 8 – Humility Before Honor

Scripture: *""The reverent and worshipful fear of the Lord brings instruction in wisdom, and humility comes before honor."(Proverbs 15:33, AMPC)*

Teaching

Proverbs ties together three powerful threads: fear of the Lord, wisdom, and humility. Solomon shows us that honor is not the starting place — it is the outcome. The pathway to honor always runs through humility.

The Hebrew word for humility here is **"anavah" (הָוֲנַע)**, which means meekness, modesty, or submission. It is not weakness; it is strength under control. Humility recognizes that wisdom is received, not manufactured. It acknowledges that every good gift, every insight, every opportunity, comes from God's hand.

Flesh resists humility. Flesh craves recognition, validation, and the shortcut to honor. Flesh says: *"Exalt yourself, push yourself forward, make sure people see you."* But wisdom whispers: *"Bow low before the Lord, and in due time He will lift you up"* (1 Peter 5:6).

Jesus modeled this perfectly. Philippians 2:7 tells us that He "made Himself nothing" — taking the form of a servant. His path to exaltation was through humility, even unto death. And now God has given Him the name above every name (Philippians 2:9).

This is why humility is a **heavenly advantage system.** While the world scrambles for recognition, those who walk in humility are lifted by the hand of God Himself. When you humble yourself under His wisdom, you can never miss your moment of honor — because the same God who gave the promise will orchestrate the promotion.

Application

Humility is not thinking less of yourself; it is thinking of yourself less. It's not denying your gifts, but acknowledging their Source.

Practical ways to walk in humility:

- **Submit to instruction.** A humble heart stays teachable, no matter how much it knows.
- **Serve willingly.** Honor flows to those who don't mind starting low.
- **Check your motives.** Ask: *"Am I doing this to be seen, or to glorify God?"*

Personal Story:

I remember working for a finance company, just trying to take care of my family while barely making ends meet. Within that company, I was promoted to a greater role with more responsibility. My typical day started at 8 a.m., but because I was committed to honoring my commitments and stewarding that opportunity well, I would arrive an hour and a half before my shift to make sure everything was ready for the day. I did that for almost a year. Then God opened the door to a new job that paid more than I had ever made before and took me all over the country. What started with humility and diligence ended with honor and promotion.

That's the power of Proverbs 15:33 in real time: humility comes before honor.

Reflection Prompts

1. Where in my life is the Spirit asking me to embrace humility instead of pushing for recognition?
2. How has God honored me in the past when I chose humility?
3. Am I truly teachable, or do I resist correction and instruction?

Prayer/Declaration

Father, I thank You that wisdom teaches me to humble myself before You. I resist the pull of pride and self-promotion. I choose the path of humility, trusting that in due time You will honor me according to Your will. I declare that my life is not built on striving for recognition, but on surrender to Your Spirit. Amen.

9

Day 9 – The Name of the Lord

Scripture: *"The name of the Lord is a strong tower; the righteous run into it and is safe, high above evil and strong."* (Proverbs 18:10, AMPC)

Teaching

Names in the Bible carried more than identification — they carried identity, character, and authority. When Solomon writes that *the name of the Lord is a strong tower*, he's not describing just a word we call God. He's describing the fullness of who He is — His covenant-keeping character, His faithfulness, His power, His presence.

In ancient Israel, towers were symbols of strength and security. A strong tower overlooked the battlefield and provided refuge during attack. To be inside the tower was to be lifted above danger, protected from enemies, and positioned with perspective. That's the imagery Solomon uses: when you run into the name of the Lord, you are lifted above the schemes of the enemy and sheltered by God's unshakable character.

The Hebrew word for "name" is **"shem"** (שֵׁם) — which carries the idea of reputation, authority, or essence. To trust in the name of the Lord is to lean on His very nature. Every covenant name of God reveals part of this strong tower:

DAY 9 - THE NAME OF THE LORD

- **Jehovah Jireh — The Lord My Provider.**
- **Jehovah Rapha — The Lord My Healer.**
- **Jehovah Shalom — The Lord My Peace.**
- **Jehovah Nissi — The Lord My Banner (Victory).**

The Spirit makes these names more than history; He makes them present reality. To the flesh, the name of the Lord may sound like mere words. But to the Spirit, it is a fortress, a legal covering, and a place of supernatural safety.

Here's the prophetic truth: **the name of the Lord is not only your refuge, it is your advantage.** While the world scrambles for security in money, power, or connections, wisdom runs to the name of the Lord and finds safety that no system can offer.

Application

To "run" into the name of the Lord means more than acknowledging Him. It means actively placing yourself under His covering when fear, temptation, or opposition comes.

- When anxiety rises, you run into **Jehovah Shalom** and receive His peace.
- When sickness attacks, you run into **Jehovah Rapha** and claim His healing.
- When lack threatens, you run into **Jehovah Jireh** and trust His provision.
- When enemies oppose you, you run into **Jehovah Nissi** and stand under His victory.

Flesh wants to build its own tower of safety — money, status, connections, pride. But every tower of flesh eventually crumbles. The Spirit calls us to run to the one tower that never falls: the name of the Lord.

Reflection Prompts

1. What "towers" have I been tempted to run to for safety instead of the name of the Lord?
2. Which covenant name of God (Provider, Healer, Peace, Victory) do I need to actively run into in this season?
3. How can I declare the name of the Lord more intentionally in my daily life?

Prayer/Declaration

Lord, I declare today that Your name is my strong tower. I refuse to run to the towers of flesh — money, power, or my own strength. I run to You. You are my peace, my healer, my provider, my victory. I am safe in You, lifted above the schemes of the enemy. I declare that no weapon formed against me shall prosper, because I am hidden in the name of the Lord. Amen.

Prophetic Word

I prophesy in the name of Jesus that you will find safety and security within **HaShem** — the Name above every other name! I decree and declare that everything that has attempted to bind you, capture you, stop you, hinder you, or afflict you will **cease** in the powerful name of Jesus. No chain can hold you, no snare can entangle you, no enemy can overtake you. For the name of the Lord is your tower, and in Him you are safe, secure, and unshakable!

10

Day 10 – Discipline as Love

Scripture: *"My son, do not despise or shrink from the chastening of the Lord [His correction by punishment or by subjection to suffering or trial]; neither be weary of or impatient about His reproof. For whom the Lord loves He corrects, even as a father corrects the son in whom he delights."* (Proverbs 3:11–12, AMPC)

Teaching

Discipline is one of the most misunderstood expressions of God's love. Our flesh equates discipline with rejection, but wisdom reveals discipline as proof of belonging.

The Hebrew word for "chastening" is **"musar"** (רָסוּמ), meaning correction, instruction, or discipline that trains. It is not about destruction; it is about development. Just as a parent disciplines a child not to harm them but to shape them, God uses discipline to form Christ within us.

The writer of Hebrews echoes this truth: *"The Lord disciplines the one He loves, and He chastens everyone He accepts as His son"* (Hebrews 12:6). Discipline is not punishment from an angry God; it is training from a loving Father. To be without discipline is not freedom — it is abandonment.

Flesh hates discipline. Flesh wants comfort, ease, and immediate gratification. Flesh interprets correction as rejection. But the Spirit empowers us to see discipline as evidence of God's delight. When God corrects you, He's not pushing you away — He's pulling you closer.

In counseling, one of the greatest goals is to help people **perceive their circumstances correctly.** Within Christian counseling, that is compounded with an even deeper task: helping people see God correctly, and helping them see themselves correctly. When perception is off, chastisement can look like calamity, and correction can feel like abandonment.

Let me be clear: **God is good.** He is not the facilitator nor the cause of evil. James 1:13 tells us plainly that God tempts no one with evil. However, God will use *all* things — even painful situations — for our benefit and growth (Romans 8:28).

The truth is, much of our chastisement and its consequences are not random punishments from God, but the natural result of our own decisions. James 1:14 says we are carried away by our own lusts, and Galatians 6:7 reminds us: *"Do not be deceived: God is not mocked, for whatever one sows, that will he also reap."* In other words, our choices have outcomes — and often, God's "chastisement" is allowing us to walk through those outcomes so that we learn and grow.

Discipline, then, is not God sending calamity. It is God lovingly using even the consequences of our choices to teach us wisdom, shape our character, and guide us back to His heart.

Counseling Story

When supporting a particular client, they shared that they felt like God was always against them. They often found themselves with "bad people," leading to toxic relationships, painful breakups, and a cycle that repeated over and over. I gently shared with them that much of what they were experiencing was decisional — they were choosing relationships that kept triggering the same traumas, causing the same breakdowns, and eventually the same breakups. I told them, *"It's not that God is against you. It's that you've been operating from a faulty belief system in how you seek companionship."* That truth opened their eyes. They realized that the discipline they were experiencing wasn't God's rejection but the natural fruit of their choices. From that session, they committed to heal their core beliefs so they could choose better in the future.

That's what Proverbs 3:11–12 teaches us: discipline is not God punishing us;

it's God using even our missteps to redirect us into wholeness.

Application

Learning to embrace discipline transforms how we walk with God.

- **Don't despise discipline.** Resisting correction hardens the heart.
- **Don't grow weary of discipline.** Sometimes God uses prolonged seasons of shaping, and it's easy to become discouraged.
- **Trust the Father's love.** His correction is not random; it is targeted to produce righteousness in you.

Reflection Prompts

1. How have I responded to God's discipline in the past — with resistance, or with surrender?
2. What current trial might actually be God's loving correction and training?
3. How does knowing discipline is rooted in love change the way I see it?

Prayer/Declaration

Father, I thank You that Your correction is evidence of Your love. I reject the lie that discipline means rejection. Teach me to see Your hand shaping me, even in trials and correction. I declare that discipline will not break me; it will build me. I am a son/daughter You delight in, and I welcome Your wisdom to train me in righteousness. Amen.

11

Day 11 – The Plans of the Heart

Scripture: *A man's mind plans his way, but the Lord directs his steps and makes them sure."* (Proverbs 16:9, AMPC)

Teaching

Planning is not a lack of faith — Scripture affirms the value of preparation and strategy. The Hebrew word for "plans" here is **"chashab" (בָּשַׁח)**, meaning to think, devise, or account. It's the work of the mind, the careful arrangement of ideas and intentions. But Solomon reminds us: no matter how well we plan, it is ultimately the Lord who directs the outcome.

The word for "directs" is **"kun" (זּוכ)**, meaning to establish, secure, or make firm. We plan the way, but God establishes the steps. In other words, our maps are valuable, but only God can confirm the path.

This truth keeps us from two extremes:

- **Pride in planning** — thinking we control everything.
- **Passivity in spirituality** — refusing to plan at all and expecting God to do everything.

Wisdom is walking in balance: plan diligently, but submit completely.
Flesh resists this balance. Flesh either overplans (trying to control out-

comes) or under-plans (living recklessly and calling it "faith"). The Spirit, however, teaches us that our role is obedience, not omniscience. The Spirit gives wisdom for planning, but also the flexibility to pivot when God redirects.

Think of Paul. He planned to go to Asia, but Acts 16:6–10 tells us the Spirit redirected him to Macedonia. His plans weren't wrong, but God's steps were better. Spirit-led planning means we prepare with excellence but remain yielded to God's adjustments.

Application

Wisdom invites us to plan — but hold our plans with open hands.

- **Plan with diligence.** Steward your goals, time, and resources well.
- **Submit your plans daily.** Invite the Lord to breathe on them and redirect where necessary.
- **Trust His reroutes.** When God interrupts your plan, it's not rejection — it's redirection.

12

Day 12 – Wise Counsel

Scripture: *"Where there is no counsel, purposes are frustrated, but with many counselors they are accomplished."* (Proverbs 11:14, AMPC)

Teaching

Wisdom is not a solo journey. Solomon tells us that without counsel, our purposes collapse. The Hebrew word for "counsel" is **"tachbulah" (תּוֹלֵבְחַת)**, meaning steering or guidance, like ropes used to direct a ship. In other words, wise counsel is the steering system that helps us navigate life's storms.

But there's a key: not all counsel is wise counsel. Flesh seeks agreement. Flesh wants people who will validate its desires, even when those desires are destructive. Spirit seeks truth — even if it stretches or corrects.

Godly counsel is not about hearing what you want; it's about aligning with God's perspective. And even when wise voices speak into your life, the Spirit must always have the final say. Wise counsel is a gift, but it should never replace the voice of God.

DAY 12 – WISE COUNSEL

Application

We need wise voices — mentors, pastors, therapists, Spirit-filled friends — to help us discern, especially in seasons of big decisions. But we also need discernment to weigh that counsel against the voice of God.

Personal Story:

When I was preparing to remarry only a year after losing my late wife, I experienced so much resistance from well-meaning individuals. They loved me, but they hadn't walked through what I had walked through. They didn't see what I was seeing in the Spirit. I wrestled — I prayed, I fasted, I sought therapy. Deep down, I knew I had heard the voice of the Lord telling me to proceed. God allowed me the space to trust His voice and make a decision in faith. Looking back, I am so glad I did. Getting remarried was the catalyst I needed to push further into the things of God.

That's the balance Proverbs points us to: wise counsel *and* Spirit-led obedience. Counsel confirms, but God's voice anchors.

Reflection Prompts

1. Do I seek wise counsel only from those who will agree with me, or from those who will stretch me?
2. How can I better balance receiving counsel with listening to the Spirit's voice?
3. What decision in my life right now needs to be weighed carefully with both counsel and prayer?

Prayer/Declaration

Father, thank You for surrounding me with voices of wisdom. Give me discernment to know the difference between wise counsel and empty opinions. Teach me to honor counsel without replacing Your voice. I declare that my life is not steered by fleshly agreement but by Spirit-led wisdom. Amen.

Prophetic Word

I decree and declare over you: You will not be led astray by false voices or swayed by the noise of man's opinions. In the name of Jesus, I prophesy clarity in your decisions and courage to trust the voice of God above every other. May every counselor you encounter be filled with wisdom, and may every step you take be ordered by the Lord.

13

Day 13 – A Cheerful Heart

Scripture: *"A happy heart is good medicine and a cheerful mind works healing, but a broken spirit dries up the bones."* (Proverbs 17:22, AMPC)

Teaching

Proverbs reveals something modern science has only recently confirmed: your inner life directly affects your physical and emotional health. A cheerful heart is more than positive thinking — it's Spirit-rooted joy that becomes medicine to your entire being.

The Hebrew word for "cheerful" is **"sameach" (שָׂמֵחַ)**, meaning glad, joyful, or merry. It points not to circumstantial happiness but to an inward disposition of joy. In contrast, a "broken spirit" (Hebrew **"nakeh ruach"**) means a stricken, wounded, or crushed spirit that drains vitality and weakens the body.

Joy is not a luxury in the kingdom — it is a necessity. Nehemiah 8:10 reminds us: *"The joy of the Lord is your strength."* Joy is a spiritual weapon that sustains you when circumstances are bleak. Flesh says joy is optional, something you experience when life is good. The Spirit says joy is foundational, something you carry even in the storm.

Jesus modeled this. Hebrews 12:2 says, *"For the joy set before Him He endured the cross."* Joy didn't remove the pain, but it gave Him strength to endure it. Spirit-born joy lifts you above circumstances and anchors you in God's goodness, no matter what.

Application

Cultivating a cheerful heart is not about faking smiles or ignoring pain. It's about choosing to align your perspective with God's truth.

Practical ways to guard joy:

- **Gratitude.** Train your heart to recognize God's hand in the small things.
- **Worship.** Joy flows when your eyes shift from problems to the presence of God.
- **Community.** Surround yourself with life-giving people. Joy is contagious, and so is despair.

Personal Story:

When I lost my late wife, what sustained me was worship. It was a dark and heavy season — I often felt like I was holding on to Jesus by the ankles just to make it through the day. Yet it was in those days of raw closeness that I learned something life-changing: a key to grief is gratitude, and the way to disarm despair is worship.

I was also blessed by the ministry of man — a strong community carried me when I didn't have the strength to stand on my own. That season taught me this truth: feel your pain, be honest about it, but in the midst of it, keep looking to Jesus. Gratitude and worship will guard your heart from despair and open you up to healing.

Reflection Prompts

1. What circumstances in my life have been trying to drain my joy?
2. How can I intentionally cultivate gratitude and cheerfulness today?
3. Who do I need to lean on in my community to keep my spirit lifted in this season?

Prayer/Declaration

Father, I thank You that joy is not optional but essential. Today I reject despair, heaviness, and hopelessness. I choose to cultivate a cheerful heart, rooted in Your Spirit and anchored in Your promises. I declare that joy is my medicine, my strength, and my inheritance in Christ. Amen.

14

Day 14 – Wisdom and Wealth

Scripture: *"Wealth [not earned but] won in haste or unjustly or from the production of things for vain or detrimental use [such riches] will dwindle away, but he who gathers little by little will increase [his riches]."* (Proverbs 13:11, AMPC)

Teaching

Proverbs doesn't shy away from the topic of money — but it always frames it through the lens of wisdom. Wealth itself is not evil, but how it is obtained and stewarded reveals the posture of the heart.

The Hebrew word for "wealth" here is **"hon"** (הוֹן), meaning substance, riches, or possessions. Solomon contrasts two approaches: wealth gained hastily (through shortcuts, dishonesty, or exploitation) versus wealth gained little by little through diligence and faithfulness.

Flesh loves shortcuts. Flesh seeks the quick win, the fast payout, the appearance of success without the process. Spirit-led wisdom values process over speed. Wisdom teaches that sustainable increase comes through steady, faithful stewardship — gathering little by little.

Jesus reinforces this principle in Luke 16:10: *"Whoever can be trusted with very little can also be trusted with much."* God often tests us with small measures before releasing greater responsibility. Wealth gained too quickly, without character to sustain it, becomes a curse instead of a blessing.

Here's the prophetic edge: **true wealth is not only measured in money but in wisdom.** Financial riches without wisdom fade. But wisdom produces wealth that endures — not just in finances, but in relationships, influence, legacy, and spiritual authority.

Application

Wisdom in wealth looks like:

- **Diligence over shortcuts.** Reject schemes and choose faithful work.
- **Stewardship over waste.** Treat even small resources with honor.
- **Generational thinking.** Build with legacy in mind, not just immediate gratification.

Personal Story:

When I was in college working on my degree, I once jokingly told my sister — who was also pursuing her degree — that I wished I could just *pay* for mine. She laughed, and every Thanksgiving after I graduated, the family would tease me with that story: *"You didn't really earn your degree; you bought it."* Of course, that was playful sibling banter. But later I reflected on how that kind of flippant shortcut mindset could have been perceived by someone like my sister — a first-year college teaching student fighting tooth and nail to earn her degree.

The truth is, I didn't buy my degree. I stayed diligent, put in the work, and earned my credentials. Looking back, the payoff was so gratifying — not only to receive the degree but to know I had persevered and finished well. That's the wisdom of Proverbs 13:11: shortcuts may look tempting in the moment, but steady diligence builds a wealth that lasts.

Reflection Prompts

1. Am I tempted to seek shortcuts instead of walking in Spirit-led diligence?
2. How can I better steward the "little" God has entrusted to me right now?
3. What kind of legacy do I want my wealth — financial, spiritual, relational — to leave behind?

Prayer/Declaration

Father, I thank You that every resource comes from You. I renounce shortcuts, greed, and hasty gain. Teach me to walk in steady diligence and Spirit-led stewardship. I declare that as I gather little by little, You will increase me, not only in finances but in wisdom, influence, and legacy. Amen.

15

Day 15 – A Soft Answer

Scripture: *"A soft answer turns away wrath, but grievous words stir up anger."* (Proverbs 15:1, AMPC)

Teaching

Words are powerful, and Solomon reminds us that not just *what* we say, but *how* we say it, determines whether conflict is defused or ignited.

The Hebrew word for "soft" is **"rak" (רַךְ)**, meaning tender, gentle, or delicate. It doesn't imply weakness but controlled strength. A soft answer is Spirit-governed speech — words chosen with wisdom, delivered with grace, carrying the weight of peace.

In contrast, "grievous words" (Hebrew **"etsev"**) mean harsh, painful, or provoking words — words that wound rather than heal. Flesh thrives on grievous words. Flesh wants to retaliate, to "win the argument," to prove a point. But the Spirit teaches us that true victory is not in domination but in restoration.

Flesh thrives on grievous words. Flesh wants to retaliate, to "win the argument," to prove a point. But the Spirit teaches us that true victory is not in domination but in restoration.

In counseling, I've often had to help people see that being loud and aggressive doesn't guarantee that you'll be heard. The *volume* of your response doesn't necessarily create impact — the *intentionality, clarity, and wisdom* of your response does. Many carry the unspoken fear: *"If I'm not loud, I won't be taken seriously."* That's a trauma response, often rooted in seasons of being ignored, dismissed, or silenced.

But wisdom teaches us a better way: release the fear that says aggression equals authority. You don't have to explode emotionally to be respected. Instead, build strong boundaries — for yourself and for others. Boundaries protect your voice so you don't feel forced to scream in order to be heard. A soft answer, grounded in Spirit-led wisdom, will always echo louder than shouting ever could.

Jesus modeled this perfectly. When confronted by accusations, He often answered softly — or sometimes not at all. His restraint revealed authority greater than anger. He could have silenced His accusers with power, but instead He chose words (or silence) that revealed the Father's heart.

Here's the kingdom principle: **a Spirit-governed tongue disarms the enemy.** Flesh escalates conflict; Spirit de-escalates it with wisdom.

Application

This proverb is deeply practical for daily life.

- **In relationships:** A gentle response can turn an argument into a conversation.
- **In leadership:** Soft answers create trust, while harsh words create resistance.
- **In spiritual warfare:** Responding in the Spirit rather than the flesh robs the enemy of fuel.

Reflection Prompts

1. How do I typically respond when I feel provoked — with flesh or with Spirit?
2. Who in my life needs me to respond with gentleness instead of retaliation?
3. How can I invite the Spirit to govern my tongue before I speak?

Prayer/Declaration

Father, I surrender my tongue to You. Forgive me for the times I've spoken in the flesh and stirred up anger. Teach me to give soft answers that reflect Your Spirit and disarm wrath. I declare that my words will not wound but heal, not provoke but bring peace. Amen.

Prophetic Word

I decree and declare that in this season, your words will be governed by the Spirit of God. Where there has been strife in your home, peace will enter through your voice. Where there has been tension in your workplace, wisdom will flow from your lips. Where the enemy has tried to stir conflict, you will disarm him with soft answers that carry heaven's authority. In the name of Jesus, may your tongue be an instrument of peace, healing, and breakthrough.

16

Day 16 – Commit Your Works

Scripture: *"Roll your works upon the Lord [commit and trust them wholly to Him]; He will cause your thoughts to become agreeable to His will, and so shall your plans be established and succeed."* (Proverbs 16:3, AMPC)

Teaching

This proverb invites us into a divine partnership: roll your works upon the Lord, and He aligns your thoughts with His will.

The Hebrew word for "commit" is **"galal"** (לָלַג), meaning to roll away or roll onto. It paints the image of transferring a heavy burden from your shoulders to another. Solomon is saying: don't just *offer* your plans to God, *roll them onto Him*— give Him the full weight.

The beauty of this proverb is in the exchange: when you roll your works onto God, He shapes your thoughts. The Hebrew word for "thoughts" is **"machashabah"** (הָבָשֲחַמ), meaning plans, purposes, or designs. God doesn't just bless your old plans; He transforms your thinking so your desires align with His will.

Flesh resists this process. Flesh wants to keep control while asking for blessing. Flesh says, *"God, here's my plan, please rubber-stamp it."* But wisdom says: *"God, here's the weight of my plan. Align my heart, reshape my thoughts, and establish only what honors You."*

Here's the truth: often, our struggle with commitment isn't a discipline issue — it's a **fear issue.** We hesitate to commit our works to God when we don't fully trust His will or His intentions toward us. At the root, fear whispers: *"What if God's plan ruins me? What if surrender costs too much? What if He withholds what I really want?"*

This is fear-based thinking, driven by FOMO (fear of missing out). And as long as we live with that suspicion, we will always hold back. We'll see God not as a loving Father but as a harsh overseer — the kid with the magnifying glass hovering over the anthill.

But Scripture comforts us with a different picture. Jesus said in Matthew 6:28–30, *"Consider the lilies of the field... if God so clothes the grass of the field, will He not much more clothe you?"*

The root of commitment is trust — believing these three truths:

1. **He is good.**
2. **He wants good for me.**
3. **He is taking me in a direction that will birth my greatest good.**

When we rest in these truths, commitment becomes less about surrendering to the unknown and more about rolling into the hands of Someone trustworthy.

Application

To commit your works to the Lord means more than prayer — it means surrender.

- **Roll it all onto Him.** Don't carry the weight of outcomes. Transfer it.
- **Allow Him to shape your thinking.** When your thoughts shift, it's evidence He's aligning you.
- **Trust His timing.** Committed plans often look different than what you envisioned, but they will always be better.

Counseling Insight: Many people feel crushed under the weight of their own plans because they're carrying what God never asked them to carry. Anxiety often reveals an uncommitted plan — one we're still holding onto instead of rolling onto Him.

Reflection Prompts

1. What plan am I holding onto tightly that God is asking me to roll onto Him?
2. How might my thoughts change if I truly surrendered this plan to the Lord?
3. Where has God proven faithful in the past when I committed my works to Him?

Prayer/Declaration

Father, I roll my works onto You today — every plan, every goal, every decision. I refuse to carry the weight alone. Align my thoughts with Your will, and establish the steps that glorify You. I declare that my success is not defined by the world but by walking in Your wisdom. Amen.

17

Day 17 – Guard your Tongue

Scripture: *"He who guards his mouth and his tongue keeps himself from troubles."* (Proverbs 21:23, AMPC)

Teaching

Solomon makes it plain: if you want fewer problems, guard your tongue.

The Hebrew word for "guards" is **"shamar" (רָמַשׁ)**, meaning to keep watch, protect, or preserve. It's the image of a watchman at the city gate, scanning for threats. Your tongue is a gate — what you allow through it determines what enters your life.

Words spoken in haste, anger, or fear invite trouble. James warns that the tongue is like a spark that can set an entire forest ablaze (James 3:5–6). Once released, words cannot be pulled back — they create realities, shape atmospheres, and often outlive the moment in which they were spoken.

Flesh loves unguarded speech. Flesh says, *"Say it now, deal with it later."* But Spirit-led wisdom slows us down. Spirit says, *"Wait. Weigh your words. Ask if they align with heaven."*

Dr. Bill Winston, a spiritual general in the faith, wrote in his book *The Law of Confession* that idle speech is speaking death — and every word we speak is a seed that will produce a harvest. That means we don't get "throwaway" words. Every word matters.

Kristyn (my wife) and I even have a running joke that keeps us calibrated. If one of us says something wild, negative, or careless, the other will immediately shout: *"CROP FAILURE!"* It's lighthearted, but it's also serious — a reminder that our speaking is warfare. With our words, we either take territory or lose ground. That's how weighty our tongue is.

Application

Guarding your tongue doesn't mean silence — it means stewardship.

- **Before speaking, ask:** *Will this bring life or invite trouble?*
- **Create pause points.** Even a deep breath before answering can allow the Spirit to govern your response.
- **Cancel careless words.** If you catch yourself speaking death, immediately declare *"CROP FAILURE!"* and reset your alignment with heaven.

Reflection Prompts

1. What kind of trouble have my words created in the past that could have been avoided?
2. How can I build stronger "pause points" before speaking?
3. What negative seeds have I spoken that I now need to uproot and cancel?

Prayer/Declaration

Father, set a guard over my mouth and keep watch over the door of my lips. Forgive me for words spoken hastily, harshly, or carelessly. Teach me to steward my tongue with wisdom so that I release life, not trouble.

Prophetic Decree:

In the name of Jesus, I declare *CROP FAILURE* over every negative word I have spoken — words rooted in fear, frustration, anger, doubt, or ignorance. I uproot every wayward seed that could produce a harvest of destruction, and I plead the blood of Jesus over my speech. From this day forward, my tongue is an instrument of life, truth, and victory. Amen.

18

Day 18 – Humility Over Pride

Scripture: *"Pride goes before destruction, and a haughty spirit before a fall."* (Proverbs 16:18, AMPC)

Teaching

This proverb is one of the most quoted — and for good reason. Pride is dangerous because it blinds us to reality. It convinces us that we are self-sufficient, above correction, and beyond accountability. And the fruit of pride is always destruction.

The Hebrew word for "pride" here is **"gaon"** (גָּאוֹן), meaning arrogance, swelling, or exaltation. It paints the image of something puffed up, inflated beyond its true size. Pride inflates us, but wisdom humbles us.

A "haughty spirit" is one that looks down on others, trusts in its own strength, and resists dependence on God. This is the exact posture of Lucifer before his fall (Isaiah 14:12–15). Pride was the root of Satan's rebellion, and it is still the root of much destruction today.

But pride doesn't always look like arrogance. A pair of spiritual leaders I love once taught me that pride can also manifest as **insecurity.** Pride is not just the inflation of your ego — it is also the deflation of your God-given identity. Insecurity is pride in disguise because it still makes *you* the focus instead of God.

An arrogant person says, *"Look at me, I don't need anyone."*
An insecure person says, *"I'm nothing, I'll do anything for validation."*
Both will lead to a fall, because both refuse to fully rest in who God is and who He says we are. Insecurity drives people to chase unhealthy relationships, compromise values, and live for the approval of man. It may look like humility, but it is actually pride wrapped in fear.

True humility is neither arrogance nor insecurity — it is confidence anchored in God. It says: *"Apart from Him I can do nothing, but in Him I am who He says I am."*

Here's the wisdom principle: **pride puts you in opposition to God; humility puts you in position for God.**

Application

- **Practice teachability.** Ask God to keep your heart open to correction.
- **Serve willingly.** Nothing kills pride like consistent service.
- **Anchor your identity.** Don't inflate with arrogance or deflate with insecurity. Rest in who God says you are.

Reflection Prompts

1. Where has pride — either arrogance or insecurity — blinded me or caused me to resist correction?
2. How is the Spirit inviting me to humble myself in this season?
3. What truths about my God-given identity do I need to embrace to walk in humility?

Prayer/Declaration

Father, search my heart and expose any pride — whether arrogance that exalts self or insecurity that denies who You say I am. I humble myself under Your mighty hand, trusting that in due time You will lift me up. I renounce defensiveness, fear, and self-sufficiency. I declare that I walk in humility, clothed with grace, and positioned for Your favor. Amen.

19

Day 19 – The Power of Generational Legacy

Scripture: *"A good man leaves an inheritance [of moral stability and goodness] to his children's children, and the wealth of the sinner finds its way eventually into the hands of the righteous, for whom it was laid up."* (Proverbs 13:22, AMPC)

Teaching

Proverbs reminds us that wisdom always thinks generationally. A good man doesn't just live for today — he leaves a legacy for his children's children. Legacy isn't accidental; it is the intentional fruit of wise living.

The Hebrew word for "inheritance" is **"nachalah" (הָלֲחַנ)**, meaning property, heritage, or possession. But notice Solomon doesn't limit this inheritance to money. He speaks of *moral stability and goodness* — values, character, and faith that are passed down just as much as wealth.

Flesh thinks short-term. Flesh says, *"As long as I'm good, that's all that matters."* Spirit thinks generationally. Spirit says, *"What I do now echoes into my children, grandchildren, and beyond."*

The second half of the verse carries a kingdom mystery: *"the wealth of the sinner is laid up for the righteous."* God is sovereign over resources, and unrighteous wealth never remains secure. In His timing, He transfers resources into the hands of the righteous for kingdom purposes. But that transfer is not random — it flows to those prepared to steward it with wisdom and integrity.

Here's the truth: **legacy is more than money — it's the values, patterns, and spiritual inheritance you leave behind.** Wealth without wisdom destroys generations, but wisdom with wealth builds them.

Application:

Generational thinking requires intentional choices:

- **Live beyond yourself.** Every decision is planting a seed for future generations.
- **Pass on more than money.** Pass down faith, discipline, love, and integrity.
- **Prepare for transfer.** Steward resources with excellence so you're ready when God shifts them into your hands.

Personal Story:

Kristyn and I are working diligently to build spiritual legacy with our children. Much to their chagrin sometimes, we drill them on scripture, call on them to pray for us, and regularly take communion and do Bible study together as a family. We do this because we understand that we're not just raising children — we are stewarding God's answers and resources. Every moment of training, even when they resist it, is a seed that will echo into their future and their children's future.

That's what Proverbs 13:22 is all about: legacy is not just what you leave in the bank, but what you build into the soul.

Reflection Prompts

1. What am I currently passing down — in habits, words, and values — to the next generation?
2. Am I only focused on personal success, or am I thinking generationally?
3. How can I begin preparing for both spiritual and financial legacy now?

DAY 19 – THE POWER OF GENERATIONAL LEGACY

Prayer/Declaration

Father, I thank You that my life is not just about me — it is about the generations after me. Teach me to live with legacy in mind. Help me to pass down not only resources but faith, character, and wisdom. I declare that the wealth of the wicked is being transferred into righteous hands, and I will steward it with integrity for Your kingdom. Amen.

20

Day 20 – The Blessing of Righteousness

Scripture: *Blessings are upon the head of the uncompromisingly righteous, but the mouth of the wicked conceals violence."*(Proverbs 10:6, AMPC)

Teaching

Righteousness is not just a private matter between you and God — it carries public weight and visible blessing. Solomon tells us that blessings rest upon the head of the righteous, like a crown that cannot be hidden.

The Hebrew word for "blessing" is **"berakah" (הָכָרְב)**, meaning prosperity, favor, or benediction. It signifies a divine endorsement — God's hand resting visibly on your life. People may not always understand it, but they will see it.

Notice that Solomon describes the righteous as *"uncompromisingly" righteous.* This means integrity that doesn't bend under pressure, faithfulness that doesn't sell out for convenience, and holiness that doesn't dilute itself to fit in. The righteous are not perfect, but they are consistent.

In contrast, the wicked speak with mouths that conceal violence — words that mask hidden agendas. Their speech may sound persuasive, but behind it lies destruction.

Here's the wisdom principle: **righteousness always attracts blessing; wickedness always breeds trouble.**

Application

Living righteously positions you under the blessing of God.

- **Choose integrity.** Even when no one is watching, righteousness matters.
- **Refuse compromise.** Don't trade your values for temporary gain.
- **Expect visible blessing.** Righteousness is not just internal; it produces external favor and opportunities.

Counseling Insight: Many people live as though compromise is harmless. But compromise erodes righteousness over time. It starts small — a shortcut here, a half-truth there — but each compromise weakens your foundation. Wisdom teaches us that integrity today is the seed of blessing tomorrow.

Reflection Prompts

1. Where am I tempted to compromise my integrity for convenience or acceptance?
2. How have I already seen the blessings of righteousness in my life?
3. What would it look like for me to live "uncompromisingly righteous" this week?

Prayer/Declaration

Father, I thank You that Your blessing rests upon the head of the righteous. Strengthen me to walk in uncompromising integrity, even under pressure. Expose and uproot every area of compromise in my heart. I declare that blessings pursue me and overtake me, because I am clothed in the righteousness of Christ and anchored in Your wisdom. Amen.

Prophetic Word

I decree and declare that blessings will rest upon your head like a crown that cannot be removed. Every attempt of the enemy to lure you into compromise will fail, for you are marked as righteous in Christ. I prophesy that favor will go before you, doors will open for you, and people will see the blessing of the Lord upon your life. Walk boldly, for the blessing of righteousness is your portion!

21

Day 21 - The Power Of Self Control

Scripture: *He who has no rule over his own spirit is like a city that is broken down and without walls."* (Proverbs 25:28, AMPC)

Teaching

In the ancient world, a city without walls was vulnerable — exposed to every enemy, thief, and invader. Walls represented security, strength, and identity. Solomon compares that image to a person without self-control. Without rule over your spirit, you are defenseless against the attacks of flesh, temptation, and the enemy.

The Hebrew word for "rule" is **"mâshal"** (לִמְשָׁמ), meaning to govern, manage, or exercise dominion. It implies leadership — not over others, but over yourself. Wisdom teaches us that self-control is not optional; it is the wall that protects everything else God has built in your life.

Flesh resists self-control. Flesh wants indulgence without limits, pleasure without restraint, words without filter. But Spirit produces self-control as one of the fruits of the Spirit (Galatians 5:22–23).

Here's the sobering truth: if self-control is a fruit of the Spirit, then living without it raises the question — are we truly allowing the Spirit to rule in us? The mark of the Spirit is not only tongues, gifts, or power, but the daily mastery of desires, emotions, and appetites.

Scripture reminds us: *"Anything that controls you is your master."* This is why Paul says in 1 Corinthians 6:12, *"I will not be mastered by anything."* If anger controls you, it is your master. If lust controls you, it is your master. If fear, money, or substances control you — they become your master.

This is why Proverbs equates a lack of self-control to a city without walls. Without Spirit-empowered mastery, we are vulnerable to invasion. But with the Spirit, we are fortified.

And here's the key: self-control is not about striving in your own strength. It is Spirit-powered mastery. By the Holy Ghost, you can silence fleshly urges, resist destructive patterns, and live disciplined in a world without boundaries.

Application

Building walls of self-control looks like:

- **Guarding appetites.** Don't let cravings rule you.
- **Mastering emotions.** Feel deeply, but don't let feelings dictate decisions.
- **Controlling speech.** Use words as tools for life, not weapons of destruction.
- **Setting boundaries.** Protect your time, energy, and focus.

Counseling Insight: Many people confuse freedom with the absence of boundaries. But true freedom is the ability to govern yourself under God's authority. Self-control doesn't restrict you; it protects you. It ensures you don't lose what you've worked so hard to build.

Reflection Prompts

1. Where am I most vulnerable because of a lack of self-control?
2. What practical boundaries do I need to set to protect my spirit, mind, and body?
3. How can I partner with the Holy Spirit daily to grow in self-control?

Prayer/Declaration

Father, thank You that self-control is a fruit of Your Spirit. Strengthen me to govern my desires, emotions, and words with wisdom. I refuse to live like a city without walls. I declare that my spirit is fortified, my life is guarded, and I walk in Spirit-empowered self-control. Amen.

22

Day 22 – The Wisdom of Patience

Scripture: *"He who is slow to anger has great understanding, but he who is hasty of spirit exposes and exalts his folly."* (Proverbs 14:29, AMPC)

Teaching

Patience is not weakness—it's wisdom in action. Solomon contrasts two people: the one slow to anger, who shows **tebunah** (הְנוּבְת)—discernment, insight, skill—and the one quick-tempered, who puts their folly on display. True patience is **skillful restraint**: choosing not to let emotions hijack your destiny.

We have to learn that patience is agreeing with **God's pace**. When you diagnose impatience, the root is usually one of two things:

1. **Rebellion**—resisting the prescriptive nature of God's will revealed in us.
2. **Fear**—believing God is dangling a carrot and moving the goalpost.

But that is not His character. God's timing doesn't torment; it **protects**. In counseling, I see this at crossroads all the time—people feel **pressured** to make a hasty decision. Hear me: God's leading is strong and assertive, **but never pushy or hasty**. Any sensation that you're **cornered**, rushed, or you **"have no choice"** is not the Spirit; it's a scheme to push you into folly.

DAY 22 – THE WISDOM OF PATIENCE

Flesh equates quick reactions with strength: *"I have to clap back; I have to defend myself."* Wisdom says: *"Pause. Let the Spirit govern."* Unprocessed anger becomes destruction; Spirit-led patience preserves destiny.

Wisdom principle: patience is not delay—it is **discernment**, a prophetic agreement with heaven's pace.

Application

- **The 24-Hour Rule:** if you feel cornered, **stop**. Do nothing for at least **24 hours**. In that window, **pray earnestly**, **reflect**, and then proceed.
- **Build a pause:** take one deep breath before responding; ask, *"Am I agreeing with God's pace or pressure's push?"*
- **Name the root:** confess rebellion or fear if present; realign with trust in God's character.

Reflection Prompts

1. Where do I feel pressured to react quickly rather than respond wisely?
2. What crossroads in my life require me to adopt the 24-hour rule right now?
3. How has waiting on God produced better outcomes in my past?

Prayer/Declaration

Father, I align with Your pace. Deliver me from rebellion against Your will and from fear that misjudges Your heart. Teach me to discern Your timing, to pause under pressure, and to act only as Your Spirit leads. I will not be ruled by haste; I will be governed by Your wisdom. In Jesus' name, amen.

Prophetic Thought

Patience is agreement with heaven's pace. You will not be rushed out of your destiny.

23

Day 23 – Guarding Against Envy

Scripture: *"A calm and undisturbed mind and heart are the life and health of the body, but envy, jealousy, and wrath are like rottenness of the bones."* (Proverbs 14:30, AMPC)

Teaching

Envy is more dangerous than we often admit. Solomon calls it *rottenness of the bones*. The Hebrew word for "envy" is **qinah (הָאִנְק)** — jealousy, zeal, rivalry. It eats from the inside out, draining life at the core.

Flesh tells us, *"If I had what they had, I'd be happy."* Spirit exposes that as a lie: comparison is a thief. Envy corrodes gratitude, blinds us to our portion, and makes us suspicious of God's goodness toward us.

A pastor once said something I've never forgotten: *"To desire someone else's life is to also desire their warfare."* Envy is shortsighted — it partners with covetousness to magnify what we think is lacking in our life while exaggerating the efficiencies in someone else's. But here's the truth: we don't know the sacrifices, the battles, or the hidden costs our neighbor endured to live where they live now.

This is why wisdom redirects our gaze. We take our eyes off what we *think* we don't have and fix them on the One who has it all. James 1:17 reminds us: *"Every good and perfect gift is from above, coming down from the Father of* lights."Gratitude heals what envy rots.

Wisdom principle: Envy will rot you, but gratitude will heal you.

Application

- Practice gratitude daily — thank God for what you already carry.
- Celebrate others — openly bless their wins to break envy's grip.
- Fix your gaze upward — remember that every good gift comes from God.

Reflection Prompts

1. Who or what am I tempted to compare myself to?
2. How has envy magnified what I "lack" while blinding me to what I carry?
3. What good and perfect gifts can I name today that prove God's faithfulness?

Prayer/Declaration

Father, deliver me from envy. Break agreement with covetousness and comparison. I choose gratitude and contentment. I bless others and celebrate what You are doing in their lives, knowing You are faithful to fulfill my story too. Amen.

Prophetic Thought

To envy another is to covet their warfare. Your story is tailor-made, and your portion is perfect in Christ.

24

Day 24 – Honoring Generational Wisdom

Scripture: *"My son, hear the instruction of your father; reject not nor forsake the teaching of your mother. For they are a garland of grace upon your head and chains and pendants of gold worn by your neck."* (Proverbs 1:8–9, AMPC)

Teaching

From the very beginning of Proverbs, Solomon roots wisdom in generational transfer. The instruction of a father and the teaching of a mother are described as **ornaments of grace and honor** — like crowns and necklaces that mark identity and worth.

The Hebrew word for "instruction" is **musar (מוּסָר)** — discipline, correction, guidance. The word for "teaching" is **torah (תּוֹרָה)** — law, direction, wisdom. Together, they represent both the *structure* and the *spirit* of family wisdom.

Honor opens doors to the grace called **favor.** But honor isn't just about respecting a position — it's also about honoring someone's **history with God.** When we dismiss the lived experiences of those who've walked before us, we cut ourselves off from wisdom that could protect us from unnecessary pain.

Kristyn and I work hard to raise our children in the fear and admonition of the Lord. Sometimes with our teenagers — and even the ones not quite teens yet — we share life wisdom that regretfully seems to fall on deaf ears.

To them, we're just "old people." But it never fails: after the dust settles, our children come back amazed and astounded at how we knew, how we had such insight. The answer is simple: **history.** Lived experience. By sharing that history, we're bridging them over pitfalls and holes we ourselves had to fall into.

Here's the wisdom principle: **honor unlocks inheritance, and inheritance multiplies favor.**

Application

- Remember: to honor wisdom is to access favor.
- Reflect on who has history with God that you can draw from today.
- Pass on your history with God to the next generation — let them inherit more than just your possessions.

Reflection Prompts

1. Who in my life carries history with God that I need to honor more intentionally?
2. Where have I resisted the wisdom of my parents, elders, or mentors?
3. What lived experiences can I share with the next generation to bridge them over pitfalls?

Prayer/Declaration

Father, thank You for those who came before me. Teach me to honor not just their position, but their history with You. Let me receive wisdom that unlocks favor, and let me pass on wisdom so my children and spiritual children can inherit more than I had. Amen.

Prophetic Thought

Honor multiplies favor. As you honor the history of those who came before, God will write a new history through you.

Day 26 – The Power of Planning

Scripture: Proverbs 21:5

Full teaching, stories, application, prophetic thoughts, and decrees completed in writing sessions.

25

Day 25 – Speaking Truth in Love

Scripture: *"Truthful lips shall be established forever, but a lying tongue is [credited] but for a moment."* (Proverbs 12:19, AMPC)

Teaching

Solomon contrasts truth and lies: truth establishes, lies evaporate. The Hebrew word for "truth" is **'emet (אֱמֶת)** — firmness, reliability, faithfulness. Truth isn't just fact; it's reality aligned with God's nature.

But how truth is wielded matters. **Truth can be a surgical instrument or a butcher's knife.** The determining factor is the heart of the one wielding it. Scripture says "The Word" — which is absolute truth — is sharper than any two-edged sword (Hebrews 4:12). Yet we've all seen people butcher others in the name of truth.

Think about it: how many surgeons haphazardly wave a scalpel? How many chefs flippantly swing their knife? None. They handle their instruments with precision, care, and purpose. **So should it be with truth.** Every time we share it, the goal is to reveal Jesus and drive out darkness in love.

Here is the real issue: in our culture, love is often seen as weak. That's an egregious misconception. Love is the most powerful force on earth. Truth without love wounds, but truth with love heals.

One of the best demonstrations of this is Jesus with the woman at the well (John 4). He spoke directly to her private life — things that could have embarrassed or shamed her — but He did it with such love that she didn't walk away wounded. She walked away **empowered.** In fact, she became the first evangelist of His ministry: *"Come see a man who told me everything I ever did."* She could not have proclaimed that if Jesus had wielded truth with shame.

Here's the wisdom principle: **truth establishes when it is wielded in love.**

Application

- Handle truth with care — never flippantly, never to wound.
- Ask yourself: "Is my use of truth revealing Jesus or just proving my point?"
- Remember: truth without love is brutality; love without truth is deception.

Reflection Prompts

1. When have I experienced truth that wounded versus truth that healed?
2. How can I grow in wielding truth skillfully, like a surgeon rather than a butcher?
3. Who in my life needs me to speak truth with love and precision?

Prayer/Declaration

Father, forgive me for times I have wielded truth recklessly. Teach me to speak truth skillfully, with love as my motive. Let my words reveal Jesus, heal wounds, and drive out darkness. Amen.

Prophetic Thought

God is sharpening your lips as a scalpel in His hand. You will speak truth that heals, restores, and reveals Jesus — not truth that shames or wounds.

26

Day 26- The Power of Planning

Scripture *"The plans of the diligent lead surely to abundance and advantage, but everyone who acts in haste comes surely to poverty."* (Proverbs 21:5, AMPC)

Teaching

Wisdom teaches us that abundance isn't an accident — it's the fruit of diligence and planning. The Hebrew word for "plans" here is **machashabah (הָבָשֲׁחַמ)**, meaning thoughts, intentions, designs. It's not about daydreaming; it's about intentional strategy.

Just like abundance isn't an accident, **failure is predictable.** There is nothing Spirit-led about doing things without vision or haphazardly. Let's consider Genesis:

- **Chapter 1** is all about God envisioning and planning the earth and everything in it.
- **Chapter 2** is about the execution of that plan.

If the God of the universe planned creation with order and intention, how much more should we steward our lives, families, and resources with wisdom?

Flesh loves impulse. It whispers, *"Do it now, figure it out later. Jump in without preparation."* But Solomon reminds us that haste leads to poverty — not just

DAY 26- THE POWER OF PLANNING

financial poverty, but poverty of peace, purpose, and legacy. Planning, on the other hand, positions us for advantage.

Don't give in to the lie that being sporadic is somehow prophetic or spiritual. There is a spontaneous nature to the Spirit, yes — but it is spontaneity within **order.** Joseph's planning in Egypt turned prophetic warning into practical salvation. God gave the vision, but wisdom created the infrastructure.

Here's the wisdom principle: **vision without planning is fantasy; planning with diligence leads to abundance.**

Application

- Write down your goals — don't just think them.
- Break vision into steps and steward them daily.
- Recognize that order is not the enemy of the Spirit — it's the environment in which He moves.

Reflection Prompts

1. Where have I mistaken being sporadic for being Spirit-led?
2. What vision has God given me that requires intentional planning right now?
3. How can I create order that allows the Spirit's spontaneity to flourish in my life?

Prayer/Declaration

Father, thank You for entrusting me with vision. Teach me to plan with wisdom and diligence. Deliver me from impulsive decisions that lead to loss. Establish my plans in Your will, and breathe on them to produce abundance. Amen.

Prophetic Thought

The Spirit is not random — He is precise. As you plan in His presence, abundance will flow, and your diligence will become a conduit for His supernatural provision.

27

Day 27 – Friendships & Iron Sharpens Iron

Scripture: *Iron sharpens iron; so one man sharpens the countenance — the character — of his friend."* (Proverbs 27:17, AMPC)

Teaching

Friendship in the kingdom is never casual — it's covenantal. Proverbs teaches us that true friends sharpen one another. The Hebrew word for "sharpen" is **chadad (חָדַד)** — to whet, to make keen, to bring to a point. Real friendship is not about flattery; it's about friction that produces growth.

Don't despise godly community. It is the enemy who works in isolation. Alone, we miss blind spots. Together, we see clearer. Sharpening isn't about judgment — it's about helping one another show up as sharp as possible in character and purpose.

Funny story: one day I was rushing to get ready for a family outing. In my haste, I put my shirt on backwards. I was halfway out the door when one of the kids said, *"Dad, your shirt is on backwards."* Of course, they all laughed at my expense, but it made me think. What would I have looked like if I had gone out in public without someone close enough to check me? That's the power of community. Isolation will have you walking around with your shirt on backwards — figuratively, and maybe even literally.

Sharpening isn't always pleasant. When iron strikes iron, sparks fly. But without it, dullness sets in. A dull blade may look fine, but it's ineffective. A dull life may look peaceful, but it lacks impact.

Here's the wisdom principle: **real friends don't dull your edge — they sharpen it.**

Application

- Thank God for the people who "check your shirt" before you step out.
- Embrace sharpening conversations instead of resisting them.
- Choose community over isolation — you weren't designed to walk this path alone.

Reflection Prompts

1. Who in my life is close enough to check me before I step out?
2. Do I resist sharpening because it makes me uncomfortable?
3. Who am I helping to sharpen in wisdom, truth, and love?

Prayer/Declaration

Lord, thank You for covenant community. Surround me with those who sharpen me and help me see what I cannot see in myself. Deliver me from isolation and dullness, and give me the courage to sharpen others with grace and love. Amen.

Prophetic Thought

God is placing you in communities that sharpen, not shame. You will not walk alone — you will walk sharpened, refined, and equipped.

28

Day 28 – God Directs the Steps

Scripture: *"A man's mind plans his way, but the Lord directs his steps and makes them sure."* (Proverbs 16:9, AMPC)

Teaching

Proverbs gives us a paradox: we plan our way, yet God directs our steps. The Hebrew word for "directs" is **kun (כּוּן)** — to establish, make firm, prepare. God doesn't just point us vaguely forward; He stabilizes our journey.

Flesh craves control: *"If I plan every detail, I can guarantee the outcome."* Wisdom says otherwise: we are called to plan responsibly, but only God makes our steps secure. Planning is stewardship; direction is divine.

Story

After my late wife went to heaven, I resolved in my heart that I would be alone. Not because I believed there was no one else for me, but because I simply didn't have the mental or emotional energy to start again. I was grieving, raising a four-year-old who had just lost her mom, and I thought, *"If this is what God allowed, then maybe He wants me to camp out here."*

But boy, was I wrong. One day after church, a good friend reminded me: *"Widowhood is just that — a neighborhood. And with neighborhoods, you can move in and move out."* That word shifted me.

God directed my steps through each season: caring for a chronically ill spouse, walking her through treatments, supporting her in transitioning to glory, navigating widowhood, and eventually into a healed, fulfilling remarriage — full of restoration and more than what was lost.

Here's the wisdom principle: **knowing why is a luxury; knowing that He will is a promise.**

Application

- Hold plans loosely; God's sovereignty never fails.
- Trust that detours are not dead ends but divine recalculations.
- Remember: if He directed your steps into a season, He will also lead you out.

Reflection Prompts

1. Where have I assumed God wanted me to "camp out" when He was actually leading me through?
2. How has God used detours to bring restoration in my life?
3. Am I willing to trade my need for answers for trust in His promises?

Prayer/Declaration

Father, I release control of my plans into Your hands. Thank You for directing my steps, even through pain, loss, and detours. Teach me to trust that You are writing a story of restoration, even when I cannot see the why. I declare that my steps are made firm in You. Amen.

DAY 28 - GOD DIRECTS THE STEPS

Prophetic Thought

The season you thought was permanent was only a neighborhood. You are moving forward into restoration and overflow, because the Lord Himself is directing your steps.

29

Day 29 – A Good Name

Scripture: *"A good name is rather to be chosen than great riches, and loving favor rather than silver and gold."* (Proverbs 22:1, KJV)

Teaching

Solomon reminds us that wealth may open doors temporarily, but character keeps them open. The Hebrew word for "name" is **shem (שֵׁם)** — not just what you're called, but your reputation, authority, and memorial. A "good name" is your credibility, your witness, your legacy.

Flesh obsesses over image: *"As long as I look successful, it doesn't matter what's underneath."* But wisdom knows the truth: image fades, reputation endures. A good name is the fruit of integrity lived consistently over time.

Another key to accessing favor is understanding that **who likes you matters.** Not in a people-pleasing way, but in a way that reflects your character: being kind, honoring your word, treating people with respect, and living with integrity. When you show up as a decent, trustworthy person, doors open that no résumé or résumé padding could force open.

Favor isn't unlocked by manipulation — it's unlocked by reputation. When your name is associated with faithfulness, humility, and consistency, both heaven and earth bear witness.

Here's the wisdom principle: **money may buy influence for a moment, but**

a good name builds legacy and favor forever.

Application

- Guard your integrity — it's worth more than silver or gold.
- Keep your word, even in small things — people notice.
- Cultivate kindness — it's often the simplest gateway to favor.

Reflection Prompts

1. What does my name mean to those closest to me right now?
2. Am I known as someone others can trust with confidence?
3. How can I show up in small ways that build lasting favor?

Prayer/Declaration

Lord, I choose a good name over riches. Establish my reputation in truth, humility, and faithfulness. Let favor rest upon me because I walk in integrity, and let my name be a testimony that points others to You. Amen.

Prophetic Thought

God is giving you favor because of your name. Your reputation will unlock doors no amount of silver or gold could purchase.

30

Day 30 – The Boldness of the Righteous

Scripture:
"The wicked flee when no one pursues them, but the [uncompromisingly] righteous are bold as a lion." (Proverbs 28:1, AMPC)

Teaching

Boldness isn't arrogance — it's confidence rooted in righteousness. Solomon contrasts the wicked and the righteous: the wicked are plagued by paranoia, running from shadows, but the righteous stand firm, fearless as lions.

The Hebrew word for "bold" here implies **confidence, security, unshakable trust.** Lions don't look over their shoulder wondering if they belong. They move with authority because it's in their nature.

Flesh tries to mimic boldness by manufacturing bravado — loud words, puffed-up egos, aggression. But true boldness doesn't come from personality; it comes from purity. It's not about being naturally extroverted — it's about being spiritually secure.

Here's the wisdom principle: **compromise steals confidence, but righteousness breeds boldness.**

When you walk uprightly before God, you can face life with fearless authority. You pray with power because your conscience is clear. You speak truth without fear of exposure. You move with confidence, not because you are flawless, but because the blood of Jesus has made you righteous.

Application

- Examine your life: are there compromises eroding your confidence?
- Step into prayer and purpose with boldness — your righteousness is in Christ.
- Stop running from shadows. Stand as a lion.

Reflection Prompts

1. Where have I allowed compromise to weaken my confidence?
2. What bold step is God calling me to take right now?
3. How does being righteous in Christ change the way I approach fear?

Prayer/Declaration

Father, thank You that in Christ I am righteous. Deliver me from every form of fear and paranoia that makes me run from shadows. I declare that I will stand bold as a lion, confident in Your righteousness and fearless in my calling. Amen.

Prophetic Decree

In the name of Jesus, I decree that **holy boldness** comes upon you right now! I break the spirit of timidity off of you. I release over you the spirit of **power, love, and a sound mind**. I declare that fear's grip is shattered and replaced by the perfected, complete, and full love of God. You will roar with confidence, move in authority, and walk in the fearless boldness of the righteous.

31

Day 31 – Wisdom Crowned

Scripture:
 "Charm is deceptive, and beauty is fleeting; but a woman who fears the Lord is to be praised. Give her of the fruit of her hands, and let her own works praise her in the gates." (Proverbs 31:30–31, AMPC)

Teaching

Proverbs ends not with abstract sayings but with a portrait of wisdom **in flesh and blood**. The Proverbs 31 woman is not just about gender or role — she is wisdom personified. She is diligence, stewardship, creativity, honor, and fear of the Lord woven into daily life.

This chapter reminds us that wisdom is not theory — it's practice. It shows up in how we build homes, steward resources, serve others, and carry ourselves with dignity. Beauty fades, charm deceives, but wisdom anchored in the fear of the Lord endures for generations.

The "fear of the Lord" — **yirah (הָאְרִי)** — awe, reverence, holy alignment — is the crown of wisdom. It's what elevates ordinary life into extraordinary legacy. The works of the wise are not hidden; they "praise her in the gates." In biblical culture, the gates were the place of authority and decision-making. That means wisdom speaks for you even when you're not in the room.

Here's the wisdom principle: **true wisdom is not just known, it is crowned**

DAY 31 – WISDOM CROWNED

in legacy.

Application

- Don't just study wisdom — embody it.
- Build rhythms of diligence, stewardship, and reverence into your daily life.
- Live so that your works speak louder than your words.

Reflection Prompts

1. Where in my life is wisdom already bearing fruit that others can see?
2. How can I cultivate rhythms that crown my life with lasting legacy?
3. What will be said of me at the "gates" — in places of influence and remembrance?

Prayer/Declaration

Father, thank You that wisdom is not theory but life. Crown my days with reverence for You. Let my works speak of Your faithfulness long after my words fade. I declare that my legacy will testify of Your wisdom through me. Amen.

Prophetic Charge

I decree in Jesus' name that wisdom will not just visit you — it will rest upon you as a crown. You will not end this journey empty; you will rise clothed in honor, dignity, and strength. Your works will speak for you in the gates, your legacy will outlive you, and generations will call you blessed.

32

Closing Words

The Way Forward

Beloved, you've just walked through *The Way of Wisdom.* Thirty-one days of listening, learning, stretching, and surrendering to the Spirit of Wisdom. You've encountered Proverbs not as ancient sayings, but as living strategy for your today and your tomorrow.

Let me remind you: this journey does not end here. Wisdom is not a 31-day sprint — it is a lifelong walk. Proverbs is not a book you visit once a year — it is a well you return to daily. Every decision, every relationship, every season is an opportunity to lean into the Spirit of Wisdom, who will never lead you astray.

Some of you came into these pages weary, confused, or stuck. Hear me: your yesterday is not greater than your tomorrow. Wisdom refuses retrogression. God is calling you forward. Every decree spoken over you in these devotionals — every prophetic charge, every counsel, every reflection — is a seed. As you continue to water those seeds in prayer and practice, they will bear fruit that transforms not only your life, but the lives of those connected to you.

I declare over you that wisdom will guard you, guide you, and grow you. You will no longer stumble blindly but walk with clarity and confidence. You will not settle for shortcuts — you will steward your process. You will not be bound by fear — you will roar with holy boldness. You will not walk in isolation —

you will thrive in sharpening community. You will not live for survival — you will build legacy.

This is your season to rise in wisdom. The Spirit of Wisdom is resting on you like a mantle. Expect new clarity. Expect new strategies. Expect new favor. Expect new doors.

And when you walk through them, let your life be a testimony: *"This is the way of wisdom — and it has led me into life."*

Beloved, keep walking. The path of the righteous grows brighter and brighter. Your crown is secure.

— Terrell Winton

33

Reader's Blessing – A Prayer of Wisdom

I pray in the name of Jesus that wise counsel will always be your portion. I pray that the Spirit of Wisdom will instruct you and teach you the way to go. May you always be a recipient of Ebenezer — the stone of help. Spirit of God, the revelation of your word makes my path clear.

Lord, thank you for the gift of wisdom that you give generously. It is the foundation for all that I do and say. My mind is sober, my heart is sober, I am free from folly and full of the life-giving wisdom of God. I wear your instructions like a crown upon my head and like a chain of gold around my neck.

Thank You, Lord, for empowering me to make the right decisions that align with Your will for my life. Thank You that Your wisdom protects me from making poor choices. Today I trust You completely — with all my heart, with all my mind, with all my being. I refuse to lean on my own thoughts, opinions, and judgments. In every way, I acknowledge you. You are my senior partner, my consultant, my director, my guide.

There is nothing better than wisdom from You, Lord. As I seek you for wisdom, I trust you will take care of me and I will be blessed. I reject ignorance, and I decree and declare that my ears are tuned to the frequency of wisdom. My eyes see wisdom. My hands work wisdom. Wisdom guides my footsteps.

Father, I humble myself before you, knowing that my ways are not your ways — and your ways are better than mine. I repent for the times I have sought my own way, and I turn now to you for wisdom in every area of my life.

I do not reject wisdom; I relish in it. Wisdom is where I draw strength. I am made wise by the Word of God. I am made wise by sound doctrine. I am made wise in worship.

I accept and manifest the wisdom of God that produces the glory of God in my life. In Jesus' mighty name — Amen.

About the Author

Terrell Winton is a certified Christian counselor, author, speaker, and facilitator devoted to equipping believers to live with clarity, healing, and purpose. Carrying both a pastoral heart and a prophetic edge, Terrell blends biblical wisdom, therapeutic insight, and real-life experience to guide others toward wholeness in Christ. His message is one of restoration—helping people heal from the past, rediscover identity, and walk confidently in divine purpose.

As the founder of **The Well**, a ministry dedicated to healing, restoration, and empowerment, Terrell has created a space for believers to encounter God's presence in a transformative way. Through gatherings, teaching, devotionals, and mentorship, The Well serves as both a spiritual refuge and an equipping ground for Kingdom living.

Terrell is the author of several life-giving works, including *The Way of Wisdom: 31 Days Through Proverbs*, *The Way of Wisdom Reflect & Coloring Book*, *Awaken: A 7-Day Devotional Journey*, *Refreshed: A Daily Devotional*, *The Upside Down Kingdom*, and *Speak! A Challenge for Your Words*. Each title carries his signature blend of faith, reflection, and practical application—empowering readers to live healed, whole, and purpose-driven lives.

His heart for the broken is further expressed through *Rise Again*, a grief counseling program that walks individuals and families through the process of loss toward renewed hope and strength. In addition, through **Ruah Counseling**, Terrell helps clients integrate faith and psychology to cultivate emotional and spiritual wellness.

Through his writing, counseling, and ministry, Terrell continues to pour out living water into every space he touches, reminding all who encounter his work of this invitation:

Come. Be Refreshed. Be Restored.

Terrell lives with his wife, Kristyn, and their children, where together they are building a legacy rooted in faith, family, and the power of God's wisdom.

Made in the USA
Middletown, DE
04 December 2025